DISCOVERING SHARKS

DONNA POTTER PARHAM · ILLUSTRATED BY JULIUS CSOTONYI

APPLESAUCE PRESS

Kennebunkport, ME

13-Digit ISBN: 978-1604336047
10-Digit ISBN: 1604336048

This book may be ordered by mail from the publisher. Please include $4.95 for postage and handling.
Please support your local bookseller first!

Books published by Cider Mill Press Book Publishers are available at special discounts
for bulk purchases in the United States by corporations, institutions, and other organizations.
For more information, please contact the publisher.

Applesauce Press is an imprint of Cider Mill Press Book Publishers
"Where good books are ready for press"
12 Spring Street
PO Box 454
Kennebunkport, Maine 04046

Visit us on the Web!
www.cidermillpress.com

Cover and interior design by Shelby Newsted
Typography: Destroy, Gipsiero, Imperfect, PMN Caecilia

Image Credits:
Illustrations on pages 42, 67, and 68 by Alexandra Lefort

Alexandra Lefort is a scientific illustrator with both a research background in planetary science—studying
geological processes of Mars and other planetary bodies – and a great passion for the conservation of wildlife on Earth.

Silhouette of eel on page 17 by Hein Nouwens/Shutterstock
Silhouettes of plantlife on pages 8, 13, 17, 19, 22, 31, 72, and 87 by laschi/Shutterstock.
Silhouettes of coral and sharks on pages 2, 34, 49, 69, 85, and 87 by yyang/Shutterstock
Silhouettes of sharks and fish on pages 5, 49, 84, 85, and 72 by sababa66/Shutterstock
All other artwork by Julius T. Csotonyi.

Printed in China

2 4 6 8 10 9 7 5 3

TABLE OF
CONTENTS

INTRODUCTION

THINK OF A SHARK

When you think of a shark, what do you picture? Perhaps you see a sleek, speedy predator, or an insatiable hunter with a frightening mouthful of vicious, jagged teeth. This book may change those images.

Animal species evolve to find and catch food, to avoid being eaten by predators, and to reproduce with their own kind. Amazingly, these three basic needs have fostered physical and behavioral adaptations that are as varied as the pouches of modern-day marsupials, the shells of snails, and the venom glands of pit vipers.

Among different shark species, we find an amazing array of variations: sharks that live in fresh water, sharks that emit their own light, sharks with heads shaped like hammers or saws or tails shaped like scythes, filter-feeding sharks that eat tiny plankton, sharks that can "walk," flat sharks that are nearly invisible against the ocean bottom, and even sharks that are parasites on the most enormous ocean animals.

Sharks live all over the world, in oceans and even in some bodies of fresh water. Some species live in all oceans, while others live only in certain locations. Tropical species inhabit warm waters, and temperate species live in the part of the ocean that's between the tropics and the cold polar seas. There are species that live near the ocean's surface; others live lower, in deeper water. Some live close to shore, and some live far from land.

WHAT IS A SHARK?

So, what is a shark, really? First, sharks are fish: cold-blooded vertebrates (animals with spinal columns) that live in water, breathe with gills, and swim with fins. Sharks are different from the fish we call the "bony fishes," though. Where bony fish (as well as mammals, birds, reptiles, and amphibians) have skeletons made of bone, a shark's skeleton is made of a tough connective tissue called cartilage. Your skeleton is made of bone, but you have cartilage in other parts of your body: in your joints, at the tip of your nose, and in your ears, for instance.

A shark's scales are different than the roundish, overlapping scales of a bony fish, too. The scales of a bony fish grow as the fish grows. In fact, if you looked closely at a bony fish scale, you'd see circular growth marks like the rings on a tree stump. On the other hand, a shark's scales are more like tiny teeth. In fact, they are called **dermal denticles**. (*Dermal* comes from the Greek term for "skin," and *denticle* comes from Latin word for "tooth.") Dermal denticles give a rough, sandpapery-like texture to a shark's skin. As a shark grows, it develops more scales.

Teeth are the tools of the trade for these predators, so they have to be sharp and strong. Sharks are constantly growing new teeth—rows and rows of them form just behind the first row of functional teeth. When a shark's tooth is worn and loose, it falls out, and a newer, sharper tooth replaces it. If you could do that you wouldn't have to worry about cavities or dentist appointments; you'd just grow a new tooth!

PARTS OF A SHARK

To identify a shark species, you need to know the names of a shark's body parts. Sharks have **dorsal fins** on top and a tail fin called a **caudal fin**. The large, paired fins closest to the shark's head are its **pectoral fins**, and a second, smaller set of paired fins farther back on its body are called **pelvic fins**. Some sharks also have a single fin far back on the underside called an **anal fin**.

Humans take in oxygen from the air. Sharks take in oxygen from the water. Unlike the in-and-out flow of air through our lungs, the flow of water over a shark's gills is one-way only. For most sharks, water goes in through the mouth; for all sharks, it goes out through the **gill slits** just behind the head. Most sharks have five pairs of gill slits, although some species have six or seven pairs.

SO MANY SHARKS!

One thing that's true of all sharks—living and extinct—is that we have a lot to learn about them. Whether it's through the discovery of new shark fossils, observations of shark behavior, or scientific experiments, researchers continue to study sharks and their place in the world.

FALCATUS
FALCATUS FALCATUS

WHEN: Carboniferous Period

LENGTH: About 6 to 12 inches

LOOK FOR: A long, forward-pointing dorsal spine, which is only on males

SCIENCE BITE: One well-preserved fossil clearly shows a female biting the dorsal spine of a male while in the act of mating. The unusual dorsal spine may have been a way for males to attract females.

These little sharks swam in schools and preyed on smaller fish and invertebrates.

Is this Falcatus eying its next meal? Tullimonstrum was a mysterious, free-swimming invertebrate with tiny teeth and stalked eyes. Smaller ones may have been prey for Falcatus, but large ones could be twice the size of these small sharks.

PREHISTORIC SHARKS

Long before mammals walked the earth—even before the first dinosaurs—fish ruled the world. Without ice at the poles, more of our planet was under water. The Devonian Period, about 420 to 360 million years ago, is sometimes called the "Age of Fishes" because of the astounding diversity of fish species that swam the vast ocean.

Sharks continued to evolve into all the amazing species we know today, as well as other species that didn't survive the environmental changes that occurred over these millions of years. Some of those extinct prehistoric species appear on the following pages, as they might have looked in a different, earlier world.

We can learn a lot about our planet's past by studying fossils: the preserved remains of plants and animals. We know that, like today, the fish of the Devonian included sharks and fishes with bony skeletons. Scientists note that, unlike our current bony fishes, modern-day sharks are remarkably similar to their long-ago ancestors. In fact, most modern-day shark groups have been around for 100 million years.

On the following pages, you'll notice some of the similarities the prehistoric sharks have to our modern-day sharks. The crow shark and the megalodon will surely make you think of modern-day white sharks, and the "eyebrow" spines of the *Hybodus* may make you think of a horn shark. Other species—like the fascinating *Falcatus*, the slithering *Xenacanthus*, and the perplexing whorl-tooth shark—are unlike anything we've ever seen in today's oceans.

MEGALODON
CARCHAROCLES MEGALODON

WHEN: Miocene Period and Pliocene Period

LENGTH: Up to 50 feet, making it the world's biggest shark—ever!

LOOK FOR: Huge, serrated teeth—some 7 inches tall

SCIENCE BITE: The enormous *Carcharocles* probably ate prehistoric whales, sea turtles, and dugongs, but not dinosaurs. This species didn't show up until after dinosaurs were extinct.

This shark's fossil teeth have been uncovered on every continent. Smaller teeth found in Central America and the southern United States are clues that the shallow prehistoric ocean between North and South America was a nursery ground for juvenile megalodons.

~16 to 2.6 million-year-old megalodon shark tooth

It doesn't look like this Platybelodon *is going to escape the mighty* Carcharocles. *An extinct relative of the elephant,* Platybelodon *was a plant-eater that stripped bark and uprooted plants with its lower pair of tusks. Like modern-day elephants, a* Platybelodon *probably used its trunk as a snorkel.*

GINSU SHARK
CRETOXYRHINA MANTELLI

WHEN: Cretaceous Period

LENGTH: Up to 24 feet

LOOK FOR: Strong teeth, coated with thick enamel, that could be nearly 3 inches long

SCIENCE BITE: "But wait—there's more!" Have you ever heard this line on a TV advertisement? It was first used in the 1970s to sell extra-sharp knives, a brand named Ginsu:

"It slices! It dices! It cuts through anything!"

After studying this shark's teeth, a fossil hunter named the shark after those famous knives. The ginsu shark's razor-sharp teeth could cut right through bone. This huge predator was the biggest shark of its time.

CLADOSELACHE
CLADOSELACHE FYLERI

WHEN: Devonian Period

LENGTH: About 4 to 6 feet

LOOK FOR: A mouth located at the tip of the head, not underneath

SCIENCE BITE: These sharks are sometimes called "branch-toothed sharks." Although not particularly sharp, each tooth had several points. Such teeth were helpful for grabbing prey, but not tearing or chewing it. This shark swallowed most of its prey whole. The size and shape of this shark, as well as its tail and fins, tell us it was capable of great bursts of speed.

Will this Cladoselache *speed away from this enormous predator or become its next meal? The huge fish, called* Dunkleosteus, *could grow up to 30 feet. It's not a shark, but belongs to a group of extinct prehistoric fishes known for their body armor. Sharp-edged bony plates served as teeth for these fearsome fish.*

Cladoselache *are the oldest shark fossils ever found. They have helped scientists learn how ancient sharks are related to modern sharks.*

COMB-SPINED SHARK
CTENACANTHUS AMBLYXIPHIAS

WHEN: Permian Period

LENGTH: About 2 feet

LOOK FOR: A tall spine in front of each dorsal fin

SCIENCE BITE: This shark's scientific name, *Ctenacanthus*, comes from the ancient Greek words for "comb" and "spine." If you could look closely at the spines on this shark, you'd see fine ribs running lengthwise. If you looked even closer, you'd see that each of these ribs is made up of tiny bead-like bumps.

A small comb-spined shark navigates shallow water in the warm Panthalassic Ocean that covered nearly 85 percent of the Earth.

XENACANTHUS
XENACANTHUS DECHENI

WHEN: Late Carboniferous and Early Permian Periods

LENGTH: About 3 feet

LOOK FOR: A long, sharp spine growing from the head of this eel-like shark

SCIENCE BITE: With the dorsal fin, tail, and anal fin joined into one long, continuous structure, *Xenacanthus* swam in S-shaped arcs, like an eel. This freshwater shark slithered among overgrown plants in murky water in search of its prey.

Its teeth were forked; each one had two tall points. With these unusual teeth, *Xenacanthus* could catch fish and crush the shells of crabs and other crustaceans.

Although a predator, the eel-like Xenacanthus *was also prey. This shark fights for its life as it struggles against* Dimetrodon, *a prehistoric, sail-finned reptile that lived long before the dinosaurs.*

HYBODUS

HYBODUS HAUFFIANUS

WHEN: Late Permian and Early Cretaceous Period

LENGTH: Up to about 6 feet

LOOK FOR: A thick spine in front of each dorsal fin on this stocky, short-snouted shark. Males grew small, curved head spines, but their function remains a mystery.

SCIENCE BITE: This shark's tall, sharp, front teeth were good for catching fast-swimming prey, such as fish and squid. Lower, more rounded teeth in the back part of the jaw were better for crushing crustacean shells.

Calcium deposits in this shark's cartilage skeleton made it harder than the skeletons of most sharks, leaving us some well-preserved fossils.

A male Hybodus *swims past a hanging garden of prehistoric sea lilies, which aren't really plants at all but animals called crinoids, related to sea stars. Some prehistoric crinoids anchored themselves to driftwood; suspended by a long stalk, the feathery arms captured tiny plankton.*

WHORL-TOOTH SHARK

HELICOPRION BESSONOVI

WHEN: Permian Period

LENGTH: About 12 feet, but some could have been twice that size

LOOK FOR: A spiral whorl of teeth

SCIENCE BITE: The tooth whorl of this shark baffled scientists for more than 100 years. How did it attach to the shark? Where did it attach? In 2013, scientists took a closer look at a whorl-tooth shark fossil. They determined that the spiral grew from the shark's lower jaw, partly covered by the gums. As older teeth coiled up, new teeth formed at the end of the spiral.

Fossil tooth whorl

When whorl-tooth shark fossils were first discovered, scientists assumed they represented a new kind of prehistoric, spiral-shelled invertebrate.

Even when experts realized the spiral was composed of shark teeth, they didn't know how—or even where—it attached to the shark. Eventually a CT scan and computer modeling provided clues. No other vertebrate, living or prehistoric, has teeth that grow in a spiral.

CROW SHARK
SQUALICORAX PRISTODONTUS

WHEN: Cretaceous Period

LENGTH: Up to 15 feet

LOOK FOR: Well-preserved fossils suggest this shark looked similar to a modern-day white shark

SCIENCE BITE: This fearsome predator preyed on other large fishes, including other sharks. Like the crows it's named for, it was also a scavenger. In fact, it even ate dinosaurs and other large, land-dwelling animals that washed out to sea.

Under different circumstances, the dinosaur that is hungrily eyeing this shark may have been its prey. Crow shark teeth have been found embedded in the bones of dinosaurs and other land-dwelling animals.

22

Off the coast of South Africa, adult white sharks find plenty of Cape fur seals to eat. Pursued by a huge white shark, this young fur seal leaps from the sea. The amazing predator explodes out of the water to snatch the fur seal in mid-air. This spectacular white shark behavior is called a breach.

FEARSOME SHARKS

In August, the chilly ocean is unusually warm, and beach towels and umbrellas dot the beach. As the sun sparkles off the sea, snorkelers, body surfers, and swimmers frolic in the waves. Board surfers dominate the breakers to the north, and to the south, kayakers glide over the many kelp beds to explore the rocky beach caves. Underneath it all, leopard sharks (*Triakis semifasciata*) calmly rest in the warm water.

At this popular beach in San Diego, California, hundreds of leopard sharks make a yearly appearance when the water is warmest. The rest of the year, they are a little deeper and farther offshore. It's a thrill to swim with these amazing ocean predators, and luckily, it's also safe for those who look and don't touch. The same can't be said for the sharks on the next few pages, which are some of the most feared in the world.

The truth is, very few species of sharks are dangerous to people. In fact, out of more than four hundred species, only twelve species are responsible for all the fatal attacks around the world. Surprised?

Sharks, for the most part, prefer to avoid people. But there are some instances where a shark believes a human is its typical prey or it feels threatened and scared and wants to protect itself.

Shark species that don't attack people are much more numerous, and many of them are discussed in this book. This section, though, is dedicated to those sharks that raise the hairs on our necks.

WHITE SHARK
COMMONLY KNOWN AS THE GREAT WHITE SHARK
CARCHARODON CARCHARIAS

WHERE: Wordwide in temperate oceans, and sometimes tropical seas

LENGTH: About 15 feet, but can reach up to 22 feet

LOOK FOR: A white belly that looks as if it was painted onto an otherwise grayish shark

SCIENCE BITE: Smaller fossil teeth found in Central America and the southern United States suggest that the shallow prehistoric ocean between North and South America was a nursery ground for this species.

When they're young—under about 6 feet—white sharks eat mostly fish. Older, bigger white sharks are powerful predators that eat seals, sea lions, dolphins, and porpoises.

Seal or surfer? Very rarely, white sharks mistake swimmers or surfers for seals and sea lions. Even though most attacks on people aren't fatal, these mistakes are responsible for this shark's bad reputation—and scary nicknames like "white death."

In the California kelp forest, an elephant seal is unaware that it has been spotted by a dangerous predator. Breeding colonies of seals and sea lions on offshore islands make the surrounding waters feeding grounds for adult white sharks.

In the shallow waters of Australia's Shark Bay, a hammerhead searches the sand for stingrays, some of its favorite prey. Meanwhile, a tiger shark pup has drawn the attention of a hungry adult tiger shark, which won't hesitate to eat the smaller member of its own species. There's not much a tiger shark won't eat.

TIGER SHARK

GALEOCERDO CUVIER

WHERE: Worldwide in warm, coastal waters

LENGTH: Up to 20 feet

LOOK FOR: A wide head and powerful body with dark, vertical stripes on the back and sides

SCIENCE BITE: Tiger sharks eat actual junk food: plastic bags, barrels, cans, and pieces of coal—apparently anything they find interesting. They also eat chickens, pigs, donkeys, and monkeys that fall off boats or go for a swim. But most of their food comes from the ocean. Besides fish and marine mammals, tiger sharks eat other sharks and rays, sea turtles, lobsters, sea snakes, and seabirds.

GREAT HAMMERHEAD
SPHYRNA MOKARRAN

WHERE: Worldwide in tropical, coastal waters

LENGTH: Usually about 12 feet, but some giants of this species have grown to 20 feet

LOOK FOR: An unmistakable wide, projecting head, with eyes at the ends and a notch in the center

SCIENCE BITE: Did you know that you give off a weak electric field? All animals do, including a shark's prey. Tiny sensory organs on a shark's snout detect electric fields at very close range. Those organs (called ampullae of Lorenzini) look like small black dots. No one knows for sure why hammerhead sharks have such unusual heads, but one advantage is that there's room on the shark's snout for more of those teeny organs.

BULL SHARK
CARCHARHINUS LEUCAS

WHERE: Worldwide in tropical and temperate waters, close to shore and into fresh water lakes and rivers

LENGTH: Up to 11 feet

LOOK FOR: A heavy-bodied, gray shark with a tall, triangular first dorsal fin and a small second dorsal fin

SCIENCE BITE: Bull sharks live in the sea and in fresh water, sometimes 2,000 miles upriver. They inhabit parts of the Amazon, Ganges, and Mississippi Rivers as well as Lake Nicaragua.

Bull shark habitats overlap areas where people live, and experts think that these aggressive sharks are responsible for many shark attacks that have been blamed on other species. If this is true, bull sharks may be even more dangerous than the mighty white shark.

Cruising the warm, clear water of the tropics, this bull shark is minding its own business—and that's what most sharks do, most of the time.

These two aggressive, open-ocean shark species—the blue and the oceanic whitetip—meet at the remains of a dead whale. Excited by the meal and the nearness of other sharks, they tear off huge mouthfuls of food.

BLUE SHARK
PRIONACE GLAUCA

WHERE: All but in the coldest oceans of the world, in open seas near the surface

LENGTH: Up to at least 12 feet

LOOK FOR: A slender, blue shark with a long snout and long, narrow pectoral fins

SCIENCE BITE: Do you like calamari? So does a hungry blue shark. It darts through a school of squid, snatching the tentacled creatures and gulping them down. Far out to sea, you might see a blue shark dorsal fin slicing the ocean surface.

OCEANIC WHITETIP

CARCHARHINUS LONGIMANUS

WHERE: Tropical and subtropical oceans, in open seas near the surface

LENGTH: Up to 13 feet

LOOK FOR: White tips on most fins, including the very large, rounded, first dorsal fin

SCIENCE BITE: To eat large prey, a whitetip bites into its meal and shakes its head, tearing off a piece of flesh. Unlike most of the species people fear most, oceanic whitetips typically live far from shore. That's probably a good thing for us. These powerful, active sharks are also aggressive—and persistent.

BLACKTIP SHARK
CARCHARHINUS LIMBATUS

WHERE: Tropical and subtropical waters, near continents and islands

LENGTH: Up to 8 feet

LOOK FOR: Black fin tips and a white band on the flank

SCIENCE BITE: This fast swimmer sometimes thrusts itself up through a school of small fish, spinning vertically and snapping at the fish as it goes. At the surface, it leaps free of the water and spins in the air—once, twice, or three times—before falling back into the sea.

The blacktip's bad reputation comes from divers who've seen this shark while spearfishing. A bleeding fish that catches a blacktip's attention excites the shark, and excited blacktips are known to harass divers. Luckily for the rest of us, they probably are not dangerous unless they get excited.

Galapagos marine iguanas are the only lizards that find their food in the sea. They usually forage for algae in the tidal zone above water, but these 2- to 3-foot-long reptiles can dive into deeper water too, where they are vulnerable to marine predators.

As a blacktip shark cruises the shallow waters of the offshore islands, a Galapagos shark is about to make a marine iguana its next meal.

GALAPAGOS SHARK
CARCHARHINUS GALAPAGENSIS

WHERE: Near tropical and subtropical islands

LENGTH: Up to 12 feet

LOOK FOR: A large, but slender, brownish-gray shark with a tall first dorsal fin and a very faint, white band on the flanks

SCIENCE BITE: Fight or flee? Even predators we fear face threats of their own—bigger sharks, for example. When a Galapagos shark feels threatened, it may attack rather than swim away. Before one of these attacks, an aggressive Galapagos shark arches its back, raises its head, and lowers its tail and pectoral fins. It twists its body as it swims. Divers know that when they see a shark acting like this, it's time to get out of the water.

BROADNOSE SEVENGILL SHARK
NOTORYNCHUS CEPEDIANUS

WHERE: Close to shore in temperate waters of the Pacific and southern Atlantic Oceans

LENGTH: About 9 feet

LOOK FOR: Seven pairs of gill slits and just one dorsal fin, far back on the body

SCIENCE BITE: Cruising slowly near the bottom of shallow water, this shark darts quickly to catch prey. Sharp, jagged teeth in the upper jaw pierce and hold prey. Wide, comb-shaped teeth in the lower jaw tear and cut. The broadnose sevengill is also a scavenger, eating animals that are already dead.

The scent of a Humboldt squid has attracted a hungry broadnose sevengill shark. This squid species can be 6 feet long and is a powerful predator itself. The alarmed squid has released a cloud of ink to distract the approaching shark. If that doesn't work, the squid will fight back with its tooth-lined suckers and sharp beak.

SAND TIGER SHARK

CARCHARIAS TAURUS

WHERE: Most temperate and tropical, coastal waters

LENGTH: Up to 11 feet

LOOK FOR: A pointy snout and rows of always-visible, jagged teeth

SCIENCE BITE: A newborn sand tiger shark is already an accomplished predator. An unborn sand tiger eats its brothers and sisters—dozens of them. Babies develop within two sacs (called uteri) inside a mother shark. Only one baby survives in each sac.

With a sudden snap of its jaws, a lemon shark makes a meal out of a colorful parrotfish. Both lemon and sandtiger sharks prey on shallow-water fishes, octopuses, and crabs.

Lemon sharks have been known to attack swimmers. Other species may be the culprits for many of the unprovoked attacks blamed on sandtiger sharks.

LEMON SHARK
NEGAPRION BREVIROSTRIS

WHERE: Shallow waters off most of North and South America, and possibly along the coast of West Africa

LENGTH: Up to 11 feet

LOOK FOR: Two widely separated dorsal fins that are about the same size

SCIENCE BITE: Sharks take in oxygen from water as it passes over their gills. Most sharks swim continuously with their mouths slightly open, so that water flows into their mouths, over their gills, and out their gill slits. But lemon sharks can rest on the bottom and actively pump water through their gills. Researchers have calculated that the sharks use more energy to pump water at "rest" than they do while swimming.

DUSKY SHARK
CARCHARHINUS OBSCURUS

WHERE: A patchy distribution near shore and far offshore in warm oceans

LENGTH: Up to 12 feet

LOOK FOR: A gray shark with backward-curving pectoral fins and a very faint white band on the flank

SCIENCE BITE: Dusky sharks migrate as ocean temperatures change seasonally. They move into temperate waters in the summer and back to tropical waters in winter. Young dusky sharks are prey for other species of big sharks. Adults are considered dangerous, but only a few dusky sharks have ever attacked people.

COPPER SHARK
CARCHARHINUS BRACHYURUS

WHERE: A patchy distribution near shore and offshore in warm oceans

LENGTH: Up to 11 feet

LOOK FOR: A slender, bronze to olive-gray shark with long pectoral fins and a white band on the flank. Another name for this shark is the "bronze whaler."

SCIENCE BITE: Juvenile copper sharks live in shallow bays and lagoons, which are nursery areas for other species of sharks too. Adults live offshore throughout the year, and near shore in the spring and summer. Sometimes hundreds of copper sharks gather to follow prey or to breed.

Attracted by a huge bait ball of sardines, a dusky shark and a copper shark meet. When ocean conditions are right, millions of these sardines, also called pilchards, migrate up the coast of South Africa from May through July. These small fish travel in vast schools that are up to 4 miles long and nearly 1 mile wide.

Working together, a pod of dolphins can round up an enormous bait ball of sardines. When this happens, other predators take advantage of the situation. Sharks, fur seals, tunas, mackerels, cormorants, and gulls dive through the bait ball, gorging themselves on the plentiful fish.

SAWBACK ANGELSHARK

SQUATINA ACULEATA

WHERE: The ocean bottom off western Africa and the Mediterranean

LENGTH: Up to 6 feet

LOOK FOR: A row of large spines down the very center of the back, above the eyes, and on the snout

SCIENCE BITE: The sawback angelshark doesn't pursue its prey; prey comes to it. Lying motionless in the mud or sand, the shark ambushes fish and other ocean animals that come close enough for it to snatch in one bite. Unfortunately, its habitat is prime fishing area, and nets that drag along the bottom accidentally catch sawback angelsharks. This species is Critically Endangered.

ENDANGERED SHARKS

Does it surprise you to know that some sharks are endangered species? Out of about five hundred species of sharks, seventy-two are Vulnerable, Endangered, or Critically Endangered. Another fourty seven species are Near Threatened. That adds up to nearly one-third of all shark species.

You might know people who don't care about what happens to sharks. Predators like sharks wouldn't get a lot of "likes" on a Facebook page, but they are an important part of our ecosystem. Just for a minute, imagine an ocean without predators. Fish and other prey that eat plants would increase in number, but they would soon eat all the plants in the sea. What would happen then? Without plants, the grazers would starve and die too.

People are far more dangerous to sharks than they are to us. We take food and other resources from the land and from the sea, and with more humans living on Earth than ever before, we have a growing impact on the oceans, including many species of sharks.

People use shark meat for food, shark skin for leather, and shark liver (a large internal organ) for oil and certain vitamins. In some parts of the world, shark fins are the main ingredient in a very expensive soup. Shark fin soup, known in China as "fish wing soup," is a delicacy traditionally served at very special occasions. The fins have no flavor of their own, but the cook combines the fins with chicken or other varieties of broth.

For fishermen around the world, shark "finning" was once a way to make a lot of money: they cut the fins off of live sharks and threw the rest of the shark away. As wealthy soup slurpers have learned more about where their "fish wings" come from, they are increasingly refusing to eat them, which is good for the shark population. The Chinese government has even announced that it will no longer serve this kind of soup at official banquets. (The United States does not allow shark finning, and some states do not allow the sale or possession of shark fins.)

Sadly, some sharks die for no reason except that they are in the wrong place at the wrong time. If you have ever been fishing, you know that when you reel in your line, you don't know what will be on the end of it. Imagine what ends up in an enormous fishing net that is dropped hundreds of feet deep into the ocean. Sharks that are accidentally caught on lines and in nets set out to catch other species are called "bycatch," and shark bycatch is a big reason some species are endangered.

Why have people let this happen? Most governments around the world do their best to manage fisheries so that shark populations aren't harmed, but regulations aren't always successful. The more we know about where our food comes from, the better decisions we can make about what to eat and what not to eat.

The International Union for Conservation of Nature—"IUCN" for short—has created a *Red List of Threatened Species* that rates endangered plant and animal species. Sharks listed as Critically Endangered are in a desperate situation, where extinction is likely. For sharks rated Vulnerable or Near Threatened, we may have more time to create a solution and ensure their survival.

ANGELSHARK
SQUATINA SQUATINA

WHERE: Once common in the seas of Europe, Scandinavia, and North Africa, but now only around the Canary Islands

LENGTH: About 6 feet

LOOK FOR: Wing-like pectoral fins that give these sharks their name

SCIENCE BITE: "Sand devil" is another name for this Critically Endangered shark. That name comes from its habit of lying on the ocean floor, partially buried in sand. In spite of their unusual appearance, angelsharks are a prized food. Fisheries around the world target various species of angelsharks, including this one. Unfortunately, many populations have been overfished. At least eleven species are endangered, and three of these—including this species—may soon be extinct.

DAGGERNOSE SHARK
ISOGOMPHODON OXYRHYNCHUS

WHERE: Shallow, coastal waters off northern South America

LENGTH: Up to around 5 feet

LOOK FOR: Small eyes and a long, flat, pointed snout

SCIENCE BITE: Daggernose sharks have probably never been numerous, but today the species is Critically Endangered, which means that it's likely to become extinct in your lifetime. The biggest problem for this species is that these sharks get tangled in floating nets set out to catch other fishes.

ZEBRA SHARK
STEGOSTOMA FASCIATUM

WHERE: The tropical Indian and Pacific Oceans in shallow, coastal waters

LENGTH: Up to about 8 feet

LOOK FOR: A tail that's as long as the rest of the shark's body

SCIENCE BITE: Zebra sharks are named for the way they look when they're young. Juveniles are marked with vertical light and dark stripes and spots. As the shark grows, its dark stripes break up into dark spots on a yellowish background.

Like many species, zebra sharks can rest on the bottom of the ocean, bringing water over the gills through a pair of openings behind their eyes called spiracles.

NATAL SHYSHARK
HAPLOBLEPHARUS KISTNASAMYI

WHERE: Every Natal shyshark in the world—and there aren't many—lives off the coast of Durban, South Africa in just 38 square miles, an area smaller than the Bronx. That makes this Critically Endangered shark particularly at risk, because pollution or other changes in this small area affect the entire species.

LENGTH: Less than 2 feet

LOOK FOR: Long, catlike eyes

SCIENCE BITE: These sharks find most of their food on the bottom of the sea. They eat fishes, crabs, and octopuses. Natal shysharks belong to a large group of sharks called the catsharks, named for their long, catlike eyes.

On a shallow reef off South Africa, two zebra sharks and a seldom-seen Natal shyshark prowl for prey. Small sharks like these can glide into cracks and crevices in their search for invertebrates like snails and lobsters.

Most young sharks look like miniature versions of their parents, but not zebra sharks. People once thought adults and juveniles were two different species.

SCALLOPED HAMMERHEAD
SPHYRNA LEWINI

WHERE: Around the world in warm waters

LENGTH: Up to 14 feet

LOOK FOR: Indentations on the head that make the front edge look wavy, or scalloped

SCIENCE BITE: Would you put a shark fin in your soup? It might not sound tasty to you, but in parts of Asia, sharkfin soup is a delicacy, and this Endangered species is one of the most desired for their fins. In 2006 nearly three million scalloped hammerheads were killed just for their fins.

The practice of shark "finning" is against the law in some countries, including the United States, but these laws can be hard to enforce. When a ship unloads its cargo of shark fins, how can a wildlife expert tell which shark species the fins came from? Now, "there's an app for that"! A new shark fin identification app uses a picture of the shark fin to tell experts the species. This might become an important tool in the fight to save endangered species of sharks.

In some places, scalloped hammerheads migrate into cooler water in the summer and back into warmer water in winter. Sometimes they form huge schools. Schooling is an unusual behavior for sharks, and experts aren't sure why this species does it.

Females give birth in shallow estuaries and bays, and the young hammerheads stay near these pupping areas until they are about two before venturing out to deeper water to join the adults.

DUMB GULPER SHARK

CENTROPHORUS HARRISSONI

WHERE: On the bottom of the sea off southeastern Australia

LENGTH: About 3 feet

LOOK FOR: A long snout, huge eyes, and a short spine at the front of each dorsal fin

SCIENCE BITE: In the 1970s, people fished for these sharks with nets off the coast of Australia. In just 33 years, these sharks could no longer be found in that fishing ground. In fact, about eighty percent of the entire species has been destroyed. Today, this Endangered species is strictly protected, but some still get caught in nets set out to catch other fishes.

GANGES RIVER SHARK
GLYPHIS GANGETICUS

WHERE: The lower reaches of the Ganges and Hooghly Rivers of India, and possibly in nearby rivers

LENGTH: Up to 7 feet

LOOK FOR: Some museum specimens originally identified as Ganges River sharks have turned out to be bull sharks. Even scientists have a hard time telling the difference. One clue is that a Ganges River shark's eyes tend to be angled just slightly more upward than a bull shark's eyes.

SCIENCE BITE: We know now that the dreaded shark of the Ganges is actually two different species: the Ganges River shark and the bull shark. For centuries people have feared this species, but it's more likely that the bull shark is to blame for most shark attacks in the rivers of India.

Though this species is protected in India, wildlife protection laws are hard to enforce. Some people still fish for Ganges River sharks to obtain their meat, fins, or jaws—which are sold as souvenirs. River pollution and dams also threaten the survival of this Critically Endangered shark.

WHITESPOTTED IZAK

HOLOHALAELURUS PUNCTATUS

WHERE: Along the bottom of the ocean in the subtropical waters of southeastern Africa and Madagascar

LENGTH: About 12 inches

LOOK FOR: White spots on its sides that give this shark its name—although they are greatly outnumbered by the regularly spaced, dark brown spots

SCIENCE BITE: The waters of southern Africa are rich in shark species, from huge white sharks to small sharks like this one. But although they were abundant in the 1960s and 70s, whitespotted izaks, now Endangered, seem to have nearly vanished in most areas.

At the edge of the deep-water channel that separates the island of Madagascar from Africa, a crocodile shark snaps up a gulper eel. The action has startled a whitespotted izak.

Crocodile sharks don't always make such wise meal choices. In the 1980s, communication companies were discouraged by the frequent and costly damage to their first deep-sea, fiber-optics cables. Shark teeth stuck in the damaged areas showed that the main culprits were crocodile sharks. After that, deep-sea cables were made with stronger coatings.

CROCODILE SHARK

PSEUDOCARCHARIAS KAMOHARAI

WHERE: Worldwide in tropical waters, usually—but not always—far from shore

LENGTH: 3 to 3.5 feet

LOOK FOR: Huge eyes, adapted for spotting prey in dim light

SCIENCE BITE: Crocodile sharks are sometimes caught on longlines and in gillnets set out to catch tuna. This species is listed as Near Threatened, because experts fear its numbers will decrease as tuna fisheries grow. "Near Threatened" means that there's still time to save this species, which is not abundant and probably never has been.

This shark's Japanese name translates to "water crocodile," a description that comes from its habit of snapping its jaws when removed from the water.

STRIPED SMOOTH-HOUND

MUSTELUS FASCIATUS

WHERE: From Argentina to Southern Brazil, close to shore

LENGTH: About 5 feet

LOOK FOR: Dark vertical bars

SCIENCE BITE: Pregnant females migrate into shallow waters to give birth, and young sharks stay there until they are large enough to avoid most predators. That strategy doesn't work when it comes to human predators. Fishermen catch pregnant females and young smooth-hounds in their nets.

In Brazil, net fishing close to shore is illegal, but enforcing the law is difficult. Experts suggest that the only hope for this species is to establish protected areas where boats and nets aren't allowed.

BROADFIN SHARK

LAMIOPSIS TEMMINCKII

WHERE: Southern Asia, near shore

LENGTH: About 5.5 feet

LOOK FOR: Broad pectoral fins that give this shark its name

SCIENCE BITE: This shark's scientific name, *Lamiopsis*, comes from the ancient Greek for "fabulous monster that feeds on man's flesh." Whoever named this shark was wrong; it is not dangerous to people. Instead, we are a danger to this Endangered species.

People fish for this shark's meat, its fins, and its liver, which is used for vitamin oil. What might be an even greater danger is the way people are changing the shark's habitat. The inshore areas that are home to this shark are being destroyed for human development, and rivers that flow into these coastal waters are often polluted.

Can a little taillight shark escape a hungry, 15-foot sixgill shark lurking in the pitch-black sea? It's just possible that the sixgill shark may be confused by the sudden spurt of blue light.

TAILLIGHT SHARK
EUPROTOMICROIDES
ZANTEDESCHIA

WHERE: South Atlantic Ocean, perhaps as deep as 1,500 feet

LENGTH: About 15 inches

LOOK FOR: A dark brown shark with rounded pectoral fins edged in white

SCIENCE BITE: There's probably a lot we don't know about this rare species. To date, only two individuals have ever been seen; both were hauled in accidentally by fishing nets.

TAILLIGHT: The taillight shark gets its name from a pouch, behind its pelvic fins, that secretes a substance that glows blue. A squirt of the glowing liquid may be a way for this unusual little shark to distract a predator and avoid being eaten.

DEEPWATER SHARKS

If you've ever been to the shore or out on a boat, you've seen the ocean, maybe even been swimming in it. If you've ever donned a mask and snorkel, you've seen even more of this watery world. Still, the part of the sea most of us know is only a tiny part of the seventy-five percent of our planet that is made up of water.

Deep below the surface, ocean creatures inhabit a complex and fascinating world where sunlight never penetrates. Far from the light of day, and hidden from the eyes of people, they manage to find food, avoid predators, and reproduce with others of their kind.

With deep-sea submersibles and remotely operated cameras, we've been able to explore some parts of the deep sea. What lives there? Giant tubeworms, basket stars, transparent squid, hatchetfish, and many other creatures, more bizarre and unexpected than anything your imagination might create, exist. Here, too, we find sharks.

Some of these deep-sea sharks live on the ocean floor; others never visit the bottom of the sea, but live their lives swimming through the perpetual midnight of the "bathypelagic" zone. As you explore the sharks in this section, you might ponder: "What sharks, and other creatures, that we haven't yet discovered, might also be living in the deep sea?"

PORTUGUESE DOGFISH

CENTROSCYMNUS COELOLEPIS

WHERE: Near the ocean floor, more than two miles below the surface of the sea, throughout much of the coastal Atlantic and Pacific Oceans—the world's deepest known shark

LENGTH: Up to about 4 feet

LOOK FOR: Flat, round, dermal denticles that might remind you of the scales of a bony fish

SCIENCE BITE: Do you use a knife and fork to cut meat? This shark has long, sharp teeth in its upper jaw that grab and hold its prey, like a fork holds your meat. The flat, bladelike teeth in the lower jaw slice off big mouthfuls. Despite its name, the Portuguese dogfish isn't only found around Portugal.

In the deep waters off the coast of Cuba, a Portuguese dogfish encounters a Bahamas sawshark looking for a meal. As the sawshark pokes around to expose bottom-dwelling prey, a glowing liquid spouts from a startled Parapandalus shrimp. The shrimp releases this light to protect itself from being eaten.

BAHAMAS SAWSHARK

PRISTIOPHORUS SCHROEDERI

WHERE: The ocean floor between Cuba, Florida, and the Bahamas, about 2,000 feet deep

LENGTH: About 2.5 feet

LOOK FOR: A pair of fingerlike feelers on this shark's "saw" that might make you think of a silly-looking moustache

SCIENCE BITE: This shark uses its feelers along the bottom of the sea floor to locate prey. With its saw, this shark can strike prey to stun or kill it. Before birth, the teeth in this shark's saw-like snout lie flat against the skin; they rotate sideways after the shark is born. When one of these teeth falls out, a new one grows, flat against the skin, and rotates out when fully developed.

SOUTHERN SLEEPER SHARK
SOMNIOSUS ANTARCTICUS

WHERE: Near the bottom of the sea in the chilly Southern Ocean, as deep as 3,600 feet

LENGTH: Up to 14 feet

LOOK FOR: Small fins and a massive body, which may be scarred from encounters with the hooked tentacles of huge squid

SCIENCE BITE: The world's largest invertebrate—the colossal squid—is no match for an adult southern sleeper shark. Or is it? This squid species grows to at least the same size as this shark, likely much larger. Scientists have found the remains of colossal squid, giant squid, and at least 17 other squid species in the stomachs of southern sleeper sharks, which are top predators in the deep Southern Ocean.

BRAMBLE SHARK
ECHINORHINUS BRUCUS

WHERE: A half a mile below the surface, where the ocean floor slopes to meet continents and islands

LENGTH: Up to 10 feet

LOOK FOR: Supersized dermal denticles scattered across its body like thorns

SCIENCE BITE: Single denticles are a half-inch wide, and sometimes several of them fuse into plates that can be an inch wide. Commercial fishermen working in deep water may at times catch a bramble shark by accident. Scientists who have examined the sharks have found fishes, smaller shark species, and crabs in the stomachs of this rare species.

FRILLED SHARK
CHLAMYDOSELACHUS ANGUINEUS

WHERE: Scattered populations around the world in deep seas, nearly a mile below the surface

LENGTH: Up to 6.5 feet

LOOK FOR: Six sets of very long gill slits, which look a bit like a frilled collar around this eel-like shark

SCIENCE BITE: Frilled sharks have lots of small teeth in one huge mouth. Each tooth has three sharp, inward-pointing prongs, adapted for grasping slippery, wriggling prey like squids and fishes. If this shark looks prehistoric, that's because it is. This species has lived on Earth for about 80 million years.

Some animals make their own light in the deep sea. Light-emitting organs may help an animal attract prey, find a mate, or even conceal itself.

The glow that a viper dogfish emits from its lower surface may match the brightness of light coming from above, preventing a predator below the shark from seeing the shark's silhouette.

Producing light can be risky, too. The light of these firefly squids has attracted the attention of hungry sharks.

VIPER DOGFISH

TRIGONOGNATHUS KABEYAI

WHERE: 1,000 feet deep in parts of the Pacific Ocean

LENGTH: 21 inches

LOOK FOR: Long, sharp, needle-like teeth

SCIENCE BITE: This ferocious little shark was only recently (1990) discovered in deep water off the coast of Japan and, later on, Hawaii. Its teeth are adapted for grabbing and holding prey, which it swallows whole.

FALSE CATSHARK

PSEUDOTRIAKIS MICRODON

WHERE: Off continents and islands, at depths of 700 to 4,900 feet

LENGTH: Over 9 feet long

LOOK FOR: A long, low, first dorsal fin, a taller second dorsal fin, and long, catlike eyes

SCIENCE BITE: Hanging over the deep ocean floor, a false catshark lurks in wait for small fish, octopus, squid, and smaller species of deepwater sharks. Its teeth are small, but there are plenty of them: 200 rows in each jaw.

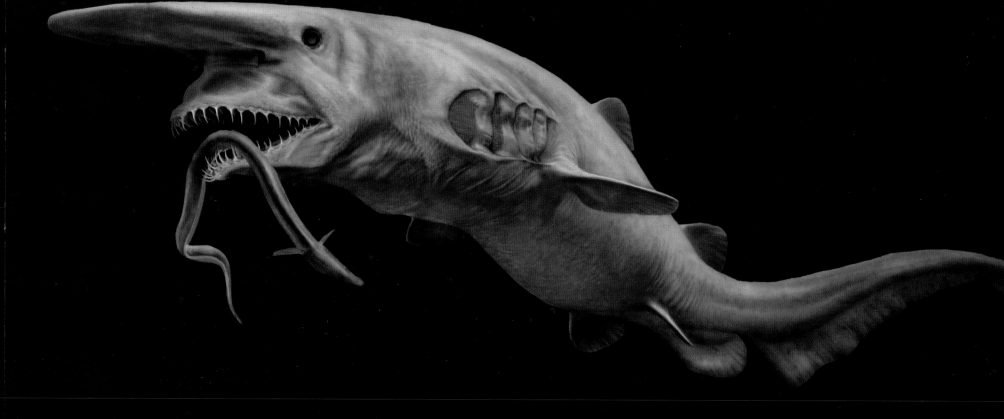

GOBLIN SHARK

MITSUKURINA OWSTONI

WHERE: Good question! Only a few hundred specimens have been reported, mostly from Japan. Goblin sharks also have been found in patches around California, Australia, Europe, Taiwan, Africa, and South America.

LENGTH: Up to 12 feet

LOOK FOR: These sharks are best known for the long, bladelike snout and protruding jaws of dead specimens. A live goblin shark looks slightly less bizarre. Unless it's in the act of capturing prey, its jaws are closed. Preserved specimens are brownish, but live goblin sharks are pale gray with a pinkish-white belly.

SCIENCE BITE: Most goblin sharks have been taken in deepwater fishing gear, so we know that they live at depths of 1,000 to 3,000 feet, and probably deeper.

You can tell something about a shark by the shape of its body. Both goblin sharks and false catsharks have soft, flabby bodies and a long upper lobe to their tail. That tells us they're slow swimmers. What aren't slow, though, are their jaws, which shoot out to snap up prey in the blink of an eye. These sharks are feasting on cutthroat eels.

BIRDBEAK DOGFISH

DEANIA CALCEA

WHERE: Depths of 1,000 feet to nearly a mile, where the ocean floor slopes to meet continents and islands

LENGTH: Up to nearly 4 feet

LOOK FOR: A long snout, large eyes, and a long, low, first dorsal fin. A grooved spine grows at the front of each dorsal fin.

SCIENCE BITE: Sunlight doesn't penetrate to the depths where these sharks live, so you might wonder why they have such large eyes. The answer lies in what they eat. These sharks prey on hatchetfish and scaly dragonfish, deepwater species that emit glowing light from organs called photophores.

ANGULAR ROUGHSHARK

OXYNOTUS CENTRINA

WHERE: Muddy and coral bottoms 200 to 2,000 feet deep, near the coastlines of the Eastern Atlantic and the Mediterranean

LENGTH: Up to about 3 feet

LOOK FOR: A thick body that's flat on the bottom and has two tall, triangular dorsal fins

SCIENCE BITE: This shark lives on the bottom of the ocean and eats marine worms, crabs, and snails. A roughshark that lived in an aquarium for two years surprised researchers when it ate nothing but the eggs of other sharks and rays. It pierced the leathery egg cases and sucked out the contents.

SALMON SHARK
LAMNA DITROPIS

WHERE: Cold to cool waters of the North Pacific Ocean—near shore or far from shore

LENGTH: Nearly 10 feet

LOOK FOR: A thick, heavy shark with dark blotches on the light-colored, lower part of the body

SCIENCE BITE: Like other fish, sharks are "cold-blooded," which means they have a body temperature about the same as the surrounding water. Not this one! Bundles of blood vessels keep a salmon shark warm. Related species share this adaptation, but a salmon shark shows the most remarkable temperature difference. In one study, these sharks were as much as 38 degrees Fahrenheit warmer than the water.

What's even more intriguing is that a salmon shark can keep its body at the same temperature whether it's in warm or cold water, a characteristic of warm-blooded mammals and birds. This adaptation helps a salmon shark swim fast enough to catch salmon and other fast-swimming fishes. It also has scientists scratching their heads as they investigate warm-blooded sharks.

SUPERLATIVES

Do you have a favorite shark species? Whether it's because of the way they look or the way they behave, certain sharks stand out among the rest. On the following pages, you'll find a world record of shark species: the biggest, the smallest, the fastest, the widest head, and the longest tail.

You'll also find sharks that are unusual because of the way they eat, the way they defend themselves, or the way they move. The sharks in this section show some of the most remarkable adaptations you'll see in sharks—you might think of them as "Super Sharks"!

BASKING SHARK

CETORHINUS MAXIMUS

WHERE: Around the world, mostly in chilly water

LENGTH: About 33 feet—the world's second-largest fish

LOOK FOR: Enormously long gill slits that almost encircle this shark's head

SCIENCE BITE: Swimming with its jaws gaped, a basking shark eats plankton: fish eggs and tiny ocean animals. Water flows into its mouth and out its gill slits, but the plankton gets stuck inside. A basking shark's stomach can hold nearly 1,100 pounds of plankton. That's the weight of a full-grown male grizzly bear.

Would you swim with a giant shark? Like other wild animals, most sharks avoid people. Whale sharks seem to be curious about us, though, and these harmless giants sometimes allow people to swim close to them. Both whale sharks and basking sharks show up at certain times of the year in specific places, including the Sea of Cortez. These giants follow their food: itty-bitty plankton.

"BIGGEST"

WHALE SHARK
RHINCODON TYPUS

WHERE: Around the world, mostly in warm water

LENGTH: The largest whale shark accurately measured was 40 feet long—the largest living fish in the world.

LOOK FOR: A broad, flat head with a wide mouth at the tip

SCIENCE BITE: This enormous shark isn't a predator; it's a filter feeder. Near the surface, a whale shark sucks in huge amounts of water to engulf plankton, small fishes, squids, and crustaceans.

TASSELLED WOBBEGONG
EUCROSSORHINUS DASYPOGON

WHERE: Shallow reefs of northern Australia through Indonesia

LENGTH: About 4 feet

LOOK FOR: An elaborate, branching fringe of skin encircling the head

SCIENCE BITE: A fringe of skin flaps may lure crabs and small fish straight into this predator's mouth. A wobbegong ambushes prey, staying motionless until its meal is near. Then, with a sudden snap of its jaws, it fills its tummy.

"MOST LIKELY TO GET STEPPED ON"

With swimmers nearby, a tasselled wobbegong hides in plain sight. These nocturnal predators sometimes lie motionless as divers approach and even photograph them. Wobbegongs belong to a group of sharks known as the carpet sharks. Can you see how they got that name?

COOKIECUTTER SHARK

ISISTIUS BRASILIENSIS

WHERE: Around the world in tropical waters

LENGTH: Up to 20 inches

LOOK FOR: Light-producing organs, a sucking mouth, and a fused plate of bladelike lower teeth

SCIENCE BITE: A cookiecutter's lower teeth are fused into a saw-like plate. This shark eats circular chunks of whales, dolphins, and large fishes. As its sucking lips fasten onto its victim, its lower teeth plunge into the flesh. With a quick wiggle and a twist, the cookiecutter carves out a plug of meat and swallows the huge mouthful as it swims away. When a cookiecutter's lower teeth become worn and loose, the entire plate comes off in one piece, and the shark swallows it. That's one way to get your calcium.

A cookiecutter shark may entice predators with its ghostly green glow, but a predator becomes prey when this little shark attacks its much-larger victim. A cookiecutter bite leaves a distinctive, circular wound. Confused cookiecutter sharks have attacked the rubber sonar domes of nuclear submarines.

MEGAMOUTH SHARK
MEGACHASMA PELAGIOS

WHERE: Probably in tropical oceans around the world, but rarely found

LENGTH: Up to at least 16 feet

LOOK FOR: A huge mouth at the tip of—not underneath—the head

SCIENCE BITE: When sailors on a Navy research boat off Hawaii pulled up their sea anchor, they were astonished to find this strange fish entangled in the line. It was 1976, and the 14-foot megamouth was the first specimen ever reported. Fewer than 60 megamouth sharks have been found—mostly dead specimens, so there's still a lot we don't know about them. Some researchers have been able to tag and videotape live megamouth sharks.

"MOST MYSTERIOUS"

Although it has more than one hundred rows of tiny teeth, a megamouth swallows its food whole, in huge gulps. This peculiar shark is a filter feeder that engulfs large amounts of krill and other animal plankton. We know this only from studying dead specimens; no one has ever actually witnessed a megamouth shark eating.

Researchers hyphothesize that the way a megamouth eats is similar to the feeding method of the mighty blue whale, another plankton-eating filter-feeder. No other shark eats the way a megamouth does.

Swimming toward its food, a megamouth opens its jaws. This creates a bit of suction that pulls water—and plankton—into its mouth.

As the shark continues to swim forward, huge amounts of water flow into its mouth. The pressure of the water stretches and expands the shark's throat like a balloon.

The shark then closes its mouth, trapping the water and plankton inside. As it squeezes its throat closed, water flows out the gill slits, and the plankton remains trapped inside.

"SMALLEST"

SMALLEYE PYGMY SHARK
SQUALIOLUS ALIAE

WHERE: Deep water in the western Pacific and Indian Oceans, near continents and islands

LENGTH: Just 8 inches—you could hold it in your hand!

LOOK FOR: Very small gill slits, a dark body, and white-tipped fins

SCIENCE BITE: You might not think that glowing would be a way to hide, but the light-producing organs on the bottom of this shark help conceal it. A would-be predator below the smalleye might not even know it's there. The shark's own light blends with the filtered sunlight coming from above and obscures its outline. Even a shark this size is a predator, as it eats smaller fish and squids.

HALMAHERA BAMBOO SHARK
HEMISCYLLIUM HALMAHERA

WHERE: Shallow coral reefs around Halmahera Island, Indonesia

LENGTH: Up to 2 feet

LOOK FOR: A slender shark with muscular, leg-like pelvic and pectoral fins, and a very long tail without much of a lower lobe

SCIENCE BITE: Can sharks walk? Bamboo sharks seem to walk or crawl on the bottom with their paired pectoral and pelvic fins. This species was discovered in 2013. Scientists first noticed sharks with markings that were different than those of other bamboo sharks. DNA tests confirmed that the Halmahera bamboo sharks were indeed a different species.

SARAWAK PYGMY SWELLSHARK

CEPHALOSCYLLIUM
SARAWAKENSIS

WHERE: Southern Asia

LENGTH: Up to 15 inches

LOOK FOR: A blotched shark that can inflate its stomach with seawater

SCIENCE BITE: When danger is near, a swellshark gulps water until its stomach is swollen. This makes the shark look much larger than it is, which is enough to discourage some predators.

A Halmahera bamboo shark creeps along a tropical reef, rippling its long tail as it goes. Nearby, a moray eel has alarmed a Sarawak pygmy swellshark. With a stomach full of water, will the swellshark look large enough to discourage the eel? If not, the eel may find that the swollen shark is stuck safely in a crevice.

When removed from the water, a startled swellshark gulps air instead of water. Fishermen say that when the shark expels the air, it sounds like a dog barking!

"WIDEST HEAD"

WINGHEAD SHARK
EUSPHYRA BLOCHII

WHERE: Shallow, coastal waters from northern Australia through southern Asia

LENGTH: Up to 6 feet

LOOK FOR: A "hammer" head that sticks out farther than the pectoral fins, nearly as wide as half the shark's total length

SCIENCE BITE: Why so wide? That's a question scientists continue to study. It might have something to do with a winghead shark's large nostrils. A wider distance between the right and left nostrils may help this shark to better locate the source of a scent.

Under the surf line, a winghead shark follows its prey. Nearby, a zebra horn shark rests on the sandy bottom, its stripes mimicking the waves of sunlight that penetrate shallow water. With their unusual head shapes, these two species certainly demonstrate that not all sharks look the same.

ZEBRA HORN SHARK

HETERODONTUS ZEBRA

WHERE: Shallow waters in oceans off northwestern Australia through eastern Asia

LENGTH: About 4 feet

LOOK FOR: A high, blunt head and ridges above the eyes—just where you might expect to see eyebrows

SCIENCE BITE: The front teeth of a horn shark's mouth are small and pointed, while the back teeth are flat crushing plates—just the kind of teeth you'd want if you ate sea urchins, crabs, snails, and sea stars.

"CUTEST"

BIGEYE THRESHER
ALOPIAS SUPERCILIOSUS

WHERE: Worldwide in tropical and temperate seas

LENGTH: Up to 16 feet

LOOK FOR: The upper lobe of this shark's remarkable tail, which is nearly as long as the rest of its body

SCIENCE BITE: With a whip of its long tail, a thresher shark stuns or kills its prey. Other times, a hungry thresher might circle a school of fish or squid, using its long tail to force its prey closer together.

The need to eat and the need to avoid being eaten have shaped some of the most amazing adaptations in the animal kingdom. In a school of neon flying squid, a hungry thresher shark smacks a squid with its long tail. Faced with this powerful predator, flying squid launch themselves out of the water and fly through the air.

SHORTFIN MAKO

ISURUS OXYRINCHUS

WHERE: Worldwide, except in very cold water

LENGTH: Up to 13 feet

LOOK FOR: A torpedo-shaped body and a tall, deeply-forked tail with a horizontal keel at the tail base

SCIENCE BITE: Makos are both sprinters and endurance athletes. They can travel 36 miles per day and keep that pace for more than a month. When they need a burst of speed to catch fast-swimming prey, they accelerate to at least 44 miles per hour.

Why is the shortfin mako airborne? Researchers hypothesize that this behavior may help dislodge parasites, such as the copepods that are attached to this mako's fins.

SHARK SIZES
LONG & SHORT

Sharks come in a variety of sizes. Use the table here to compare shark lengths to objects you already know. Or, use a tape measure or ruler to measure some things around your home. *Which sharks would fit in your bedroom?*

SHARK LENGTH	COMPARE TO . . .
6 inches	**The length of a dollar bill**
8 inches	**The length of a new pencil or a toothbrush**
12 inches	**A ruler, or the length of a foot-long sub sandwich**
15 inches	**The length of an average board-game box**
2 feet	**The height of a low T-ball Tee**
3 feet	**A yardstick, or the width of the base path on a baseball field**
4 feet	**The depth of an NHL ice hockey goal**
5 feet	**One inch longer than the height of Olympic gymnast Gabby Douglas**
6 feet	**One inch shorter than the heights of athletes Tiger Woods, Venus Williams, and Roger Federer**
7 feet	**The height of a standard-size garage door**

8 feet	The length of a single square in a four-square court
9 feet	The length of a standard hopscotch court
10 feet	The distance from the ground to the crossbar of a goal post in NFL football
11 feet	The length of a four-person Smart Car
12 feet	Just under the length of a MINI Cooper, or the minimum width of a freeway lane in California
13 feet	The length of a Ford Fiesta
14 feet	The length of a Volkswagon Beetle or a Jeep Wrangler
15 feet	The length of a Jeep Cherokee
16 feet	The length of a four-square court
17 feet	The length of a Range Rover
18 feet	The length of two ping-pong tables, end to end
19 feet	The distance from the free-throw line to the out-of-bounds line under the basket in basketball
20 feet	The length of a Dodge Ram or Toyota Tundra pickup truck
21 feet	The width of an American Youth Soccer Organization (AYSO) U10 soccer goal
33 feet	Longer than the distance between the goal line and the 30-yard line on a football field
40 feet	Almost as long as a school bus
50 feet	The distance from the pitcher's mound to home plate on a Little League baseball field

Index

About the Author

Donna Potter Parham is a Science Writer who has spent more than 30 years learning and writing about animals and habitats for SeaWorld San Diego and San Diego Zoo Global. While earning a Bachelor of Science in biology at San Diego State University, Donna discovered the joy of sharing what she learned with others. She went on to achieve a Science and Technical Writing Certificate and an MBA, but learning about the natural world remains her passion. She lives with her husband and two teenagers in San Diego, where she enjoys hiking, gardening, and floating in the shark-infested waters of the Pacific Ocean.

About the Illustrator

Julius Csotonyi is one of the world's most high-profile and talented contemporary scientific illustrators. His considerable academic expertise informs his stunning, dynamic art. He has created life-sized dinosaur murals for the Royal Ontario Museum and for the Dinosaur Hall at the Natural History Museum of Los Angeles County as well as most of the artwork for the new Hall of Paleontology at the Houston Museum of Natural Science. He lives in Canada.

About Applesauce Press
What kid doesn't love Applesauce!?

Good ideas ripen with time. From seed to harvest, Applesauce Press crafts books with beautiful designs, creative formats, and kid-friendly information on a variety of topics. Like our parent company, Cider Mill Press Book Publishers, our press bears fruit twice a year, publishing a new crop of titles each spring and fall.

"Where Good Books Are Ready for Press"

Visit us on the web at
www.cidermillpress.com
or write to us at
PO Box 454
12 Spring Street
Kennebunkport, ME 04046